RICHARD ENGLAND

Edwin Heathcote

RICHARD ENGLAND

WILEY-ACADEMY

Photographic credits

John Arthur Studio pp 61 top, 78-9, 106-7, 113-4, 126; Peter Bartolo Parnis Back Cover, pp 33-5, 37, 53 bottom, 45-7, 59, 63-4, 66-7, 70, 71 top, 74, 88, 90-5; John Bethell pp 17 bottom, 18, 20, 22; Simon Brown pp 43 top, 55; Joseph Cassar pp 81, 109 bottom; Anthony Cassar Desain pp 37 bottom, 42, 69 bottom, 71 bottom, 96-103, 126; Daniel Cilia pp 7-10, 36; Custom Lab p 57; Richard England Cover, pp 7 bottom rhs, 13-14, 17 top, 19-21, 23, 25, 27-30, 38, 40-1, 49-54, 56, 69 top, 73, 85; David Pisani pp 39, 64 top lhs, 72, 75, 86, 126; Carmel H Psaila p 37 top; Joseph A Vella p 31 bottom. Renderings, Jock Bevan. Selected Works, p 126: Richard England 4, 6, 13, 15; John Arthur Studio 1-2, 5, 8-9, 12, 17, 20; Anthony Cassar Desain 10-11, 16, 19; Joseph Cassar 21.

All drawings are by Richard England and come from the architect's archive.

Cover: Ir-Razzett ta' Sandrina, *pool area;* Back Cover: 'White Shadows' sculpture, Sliema
Page 1: Village of Kercem, Gozo, Malta: *Drawing by Richard England*
Page 2: St James Cavalier Centre for Creativity, Valletta, Malta. Main Exhibition hall. *End vault under original gun ramp. Second World War staircase on right-hand side*
Page 5: Citadel of Gozo, Malta: *Drawing by Richard England*

First published in Great Britain in 2002 by
WILEY-ACADEMY
a division of
JOHN WILEY & SONS

ISBN: 0-470-84321-7

Other Wiley Editorial Offices

John Wiley & Sons Inc., 111 River Street, Hoboken, NJ 07030, USA

Jossey-Bass, 989 Market Street, San Francisco, CA 94103-1741, USA

Wiley-VCH Verlag GmbH, Boschstr. 12, D-69469 Weinheim, Germany

John Wiley & Sons Australia Ltd, 33 Park Road, Milton, Queensland 4064, Australia

John Wiley & Sons (Asia) Pte Ltd, 2 Clementi Loop #02-01, Jin Xing Distripark, Singapore 129809

John Wiley & Sons Canada Ltd, 22 Worcester Road, Etobicoke, Ontario, Canada M9W 1L1

Design and Prepress: ARTMEDIA PRESS Ltd, London

Printed and bound in Italy

CONTENTS

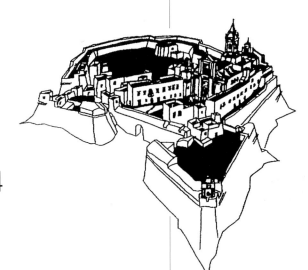

INTRODUCTION

On the stone monoliths had been inscribed the original words of the initiators of the new civilisation – words that had the brevity and authority of universal laws. They were words of a language that he couldn't decode, a language no longer spoken …They crossed the shining open spaces and came to an array of streets. The houses, buildings and offices were all majestic, and all of stone, but it was of a stone that seemed in a permanent state of dreaming.
As he passed them he felt that one day he would understand their dreams.[1]

Ben Okri's visionary words from his description of the city of the invisibles in *Astonishing the Gods* sheds light on two pivotal aspects of the Maltese architecture of Richard England: the ideas of stones that dream and of the forgotten language of a vanished culture. When I arrived at a hotel in Malta on a trip to study England's work, I found the architect had left me a volume of poetry by Okri alongside a number of books of his own poetry and drawings, and a book on the remarkable Neolithic ruins of Malta. This latter book features an essay by England that concludes with a poem, the last two stanzas of which read:

> awake these stones once more today
> from their tranquil sleep of death
> restore the secret of their cults
> and embrace again their vast galactic plan
>
> ask them that they return anew to man
> his harmonious presence in this World
> that he may find once more his peace
> and learn to love again[2]

Walking around the astonishing temples of Malta's early inhabitants it is impossible not to feel that something has been lost. We can barely begin to speculate on the nature and meaning of these complex structures, of the massive, silent stones of a lost era. Why did these temple builders, who erected the earliest complex stone structures yet found, choose this tiny set of islands in the Mediterranean? Is there something about the rocks, the isolation, the sun, the magnificent position, which made them feel that this was a sacred place? This seems almost certain. Since then, few artists have injected as much energy and passion into a quest for the poetry and magic that inspired these pioneers of early architecture as Richard England has. And few architects have attempted so thoroughly to reconcile the ill-understood magic of *genius loci* and the architectural strains of the timeless, the vernacular and the modern.

Through architecture, art and poetry, Richard England has been consistently exploring the nature of Malta over the last five decades. The architecture of the islands had been, at least until the explosion of tourist development in the 1960s, remarkably coherent. Its coherence was based on not only a self-effacing vernacular tectonic language and a few, relatively unchanging and simple architectural devices and modes of expression, but on the subtle golden glow that comes from its essence – the local Maltese limestone. The first place the architect took me to on the islands of which he is so proud was not one of his own buildings but a quarry. The stones of Malta contain the island's history and its future. From the Neolithic temples to the bastions built by the Knights of St John, from the gridded streets of Valletta to the huge churches that seem so incongruous for such small congregations, all share their most basic building blocks, and consequently their mass, colour and texture are tied to the earth upon which they stand. England has said that 'What is here in Malta today has always been here. It has only been remodelled',[3] and it is this most basic of building materials that seems to bear out this idea most eloquently. For England, the stone also acts as a container of the islands' history and, as he has said: 'To know a place one must know its memories'.[4]

MEMORIES AND PLACE

England's architecture is intimately connected to the island that is his home. However another level of connection exists – that to the site, what is so often referred to as 'genius loci' (literally, spirit of the place). Although it may seem a truism that architects should do what Frank Lloyd Wright exhorted them to – make a building love the ground upon which it stands – it is a truism that has often been neglected throughout the recent history of architecture.

> Modern architecture has spent too much time studying joints in building, most of the time forgetting the most important joint of all: that of the building itself to its site. The architect must remember that there is a time to be bold, but more often there is a time to be humble. If the architect is a sensitive one, then the Voices of the Site will tell him whether the environment is weak and this requires him to be strong and dominant; or strong and that he in turn should be docile and subservient.[5]

Tadao Ando, writing about his architecture in Japan, has reached similar conclusions suggesting, in 1991, that: 'The presence of

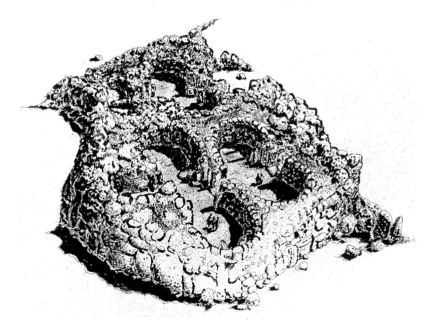

TOP: Neolithic temple Hagar Qim, 3000 BC

BOTTOM LEFT: Neolithic temple Ggantija, Gozo, 3000 BC. *Drawing by Richard England*

BOTTOM RIGHT: Neolithic temple Mnajdra, 3000 BC

Left: Limestone quarry, Malta
Opposite top: Malta townscape. *Drawing by Richard England*
Opposite bottom: Island of Gozo townscape

architecture – regardless of its self-contained character – inevitably creates a new landscape. This implies the necessity of discovering the architecture which the site itself is seeking.'[6]

In recent years, however, perhaps no one has expressed the importance of the site and the memories of the land with more conviction and poetry than Hungarian architect Imre Makovecz. A passionate opponent of the idea of an International Style, an architecture that denies boundaries, he says:

> The individual, community, homeland and the world: To us these notions are like petals on a flower from a single stem, overlapping like a rose, each one separate, but not interchangeable and bound to their position in the whole.
> Thus our architecture is bound to man, place, landscape, native country, Europe and the Earth.
> Our buildings evoke an ancient, often dark atmosphere, the murmuring of long dead beings can be heard from the walls, our domes cover us like the sky ... our ancestors, chased out of our consciousness, surge forward to speak to us, to assist us in the building of what we believe to belong to this place, to be genuinely our own.[7]

What Makovecz points out, and what is often forgotten about the idea of *genius loci*, is that the spirits of a site may not always be benevolent. There is a darkness in the past, in the memories of the dead, which can cast shadows over a building but are as necessary to its connection with the landscape and the community as any other aspect of its design. It is impossible for us to know what went on in Malta's remarkable temples – we can but feebly speculate – but there seems to have been a lost knowledge, the Atlantean memory of a civilisation lost in time, a knowledge of something we cannot recover. In his poem '*Island: A Poem for Seeing*' a paean to the tiny island of Filfla, England touches on these themes and on the darkness inherent in these memories:

YESTERDAY
WE WALKED HAND IN HAND
ACROSS TIME'S LONG WORN TRACKS
WHERE ONCE A TEMPLE STOOD
OF LINES CURVING INTO SECRET CIRCLES
AND MAN KNELT IN PRAYER
YOUR HANDS AND MINE
REACHED ACROSS THE WATERS
TO CARESS AN OUTCAST ROCK
ICON OF SOLITUDE
ALTAR OF SACRIFICE
CRUCIFIED AGAINST THE SKY
IN A SEA DEVOID OF LOGIC
AN ISLAND BURNED BUT NOT CONSUMED

TODAY
I SIT AND WATCH
A LONELY ISLAND ROCK
AWAITING YOUR RETURN
IN HYPNOTIC TRANCE
MIDWAY BETWEEN WAKING AND SLEEPING
IN PETRIFIED VISION AND OSSIFIED DREAM
I HOLD THE HAND OF ABSENCE [8]

Top: Maltese farmhouse
Centre: Maltese townscape
Bottom: Richard England drawing of Maltese townscape

Like many other architects before him, England was profoundly influenced by the oriental notion of Yin and Yang, which passed into our culture via Zoroastrianism and Christian notions of good and evil. He visited Japan to study temples and gardens. In the powerful sun of the Mediterranean, notions of darkness and light can be bleached away, and this is what happened in Modernism, an architecture dedicated to light and transparency which forgot to cater for darkness, for the subconscious, the dream-world and the private. Yet, in art at least, it was always there. The dazzling white screens and arcades of England's buildings have been compared to the haunting townscapes of De Chirico, and in these paintings there is evidence of the power of suggestion inherent in the shadows of a city. Something unspecific, whether anxiety, guilt or fear, is always lurking beneath those arches and just outside the frame in structures that cast shadows but which exert no physical presence within the frame. At their best, England's buildings provide shelter for the imagination – nooks and crannies to nourish the subconscious, dreaming mind away from the view of the crowd – and they accommodate the dualities of life. In these shadows are to be found the memories of the city's past.

Aldo Rossi, in his *The Architecture of the City*, expresses the idea that, 'With time, the city grows upon itself; it acquires a consciousness and memory …There are people who do not like a place because it is associated with some ominous moment in their lives; others attribute an auspicious character to a place. All these experiences, their sum, constitute a city.'[9] Architecture is desirous of the ominous as well as the joyous. England's poetry and his buildings, Makovecz's lyrical words, Okri's fabulous imagined city, De Chirico's townscapes and Rossi's urban theory all acknowledge the role of memory and darkness.

LIGHT AND SILENCE

In a lecture in Zurich in 1969, Louis Kahn made the link between light and silence: 'I turn to light, the giver of all presences. By will. By law. You can say the light, the giver of all presences, is the maker of material, and the material was made to cast a shadow, and the shadow belongs to the light …'[10] At this point he tails off. England is particularly keen on quoting Le Corbusier's dictum that architecture is 'the masterly, correct and magnificent play of masses brought together in light'. Light played a key role in the development of modern architecture, and it would be no exaggeration to say that it was almost worshipped. In the Mediterranean and in Malta's harsh climate though, there is a more complex relationship with light than in Kahn's North America or Corb's Paris. The light is both lover and enemy, its searing heat to be avoided, as it is in traditional houses with courtyards and darkened, shuttered rooms, but also embraced in external aspects, the form, massing and shadows of which are created and caressed by its rays. The Garden for

Myriam, the Aquasun Lido, the church of Manikata – these are buildings it is hard to imagine on a cloudy day, they thrive off the sun. Their richly modelled forms and deep, dark shadows come alive when the light is at its brightest, the contrasts at their strongest. In England's sketches[11] we see again the love of contrast, the Mediterranean eye for deep shadow and intense whiteness. In the quick sketches of Malta's deeply modelled Baroque churches, or of the monastery on Mount Athos in Greece, in townscapes of Jerusalem, Mecca or Petra, we can see the same sensibility as becomes visible in England's designs for Manikata or A Garden for Myriam – the desire to create microcosmic cities out of light and shade, mass and void. In the piled-up cityscapes of Malta, Baghdad or Nazareth there is the same massing of seemingly random, teeming urban forms, houses and individual buildings coming together to create a single, organic entity in the way that a mass of people becomes a crowd that reacts as a body as well as a collection of bodies.

In all these cityscapes, from the Middle East to the Mediterranean, for much of the day the heat is too intense for these spaces, facades or panoramas to be enjoyed, so it is when they are at their most powerful architecturally that they are also at their most silent. In 1983 England published a book entitled *In Search of Silent Spaces*. A blend of collage, photography, poetry and architecture, it is about contrasts in tone and form, about light and shadow and the silence contained therein.

The book concludes with a poem:

SILENCE
IN SILENT SPACES
TO QUIETEN THE MIND
TO CALM THE BODY
TO COMPOSE THE SPIRIT
DIALOGUES OF SILENCE
BRIDGES OF COMMUNICATION
CONVERSATIONS OF CONTACT

SILENCE
SILENCE
SILENCE

NOT SEEN WITH THE EYE
FELT ONLY BY THE HEART
YET HEARD BY THE SOUL
IN HUSHED REFLECTION
IN CENTRED THOUGHT
MAN MEETS SELF
IN SILENT SPACES
SILENCE [12]

Silence in the world of Richard England seems to present itself as the legacy of a lost knowledge or a lost place. In silence, he seems to suggest, we can find the space to remember what has been or what might have been. England's architecture is a memorial to the archetypes that dwell within us to indicate that, once, there was a great civilisation which has been lost – in its place is the silence which England articulates so richly. He poetically suggests that the legacy of that lost civilisation, that Atlantean source of all our archetypes, is in the shadows and the silence of the stones of Malta:

Ancient Island
prisoner of eternity
carnal relic of a fallen city
tamed by the layers of centuries
a traveller returned from forbidden thresholds of desire.

Although you belong to one time and I to another
I see and contemplate in veiled oscillating light
visions of sleep-walking maidens on bone-grained shores
washed by dripping tears of water-coloured skies
illicit dreams from death's eternal sleep.

The legend says that when a city died
this isle was born
under a waning sky of sorrow
it's siren song remains unsung
quiescent music hushed into muted silence.

On some days I am sure I hear in a far distant murmur
as the sea forever breaks its waves against this rock
the sound of crying voices in a never-ending chant of death.[13]

Notes
1. Ben Okri, *Astonishing the Gods* (London: Phoenix, 1995), p 36.
2. Anton Mifsud and Charles Savona-Ventura (eds) *Facets of Maltese Prehistory* (Malta: Prehistoric Society of Malta, 1999), p 148.
3. Maurizio Vitta, *Richard England: the Spirit of Place* (Milano: L'Arca Edizioni, 1998), p 10.
4 *Ibid*, p 9.
5 Richard England, *Transactions 9* (London: RIBA Magazines Ltd, 1986), p 86.
6. Charles Jencks and Karl Kropf (eds), *Theories and Manifestoes of Contemporary Architecture* (London: Academy Editions, 1997), p 258.
7. Edwin Heathcote, *Imre Makovecz: The Wings of the Soul* (London: Academy Editions, 1997), p 7.
8. Richard England, *Island: A Poem for Seeing* (Malta: MRSM Publications, 1980), p 23.
9. Aldo Rossi, *The Architecture of the City* (Cambridge, Mass,: MIT, 1982), p 21.
10. Heinz Rowner (ed), *Louis I Kahn: Complete Works* (Zurich: Birkhauser, 1987), p 54.
11. Richard England, *Sacri Luoghi* (Melfi, Italy: LIBRiA, 1997) provides the best collection.
12. Richard England, *In Search of Silent Spaces* (Malta: MRSM Publications, 1983).
13. Richard England, 'Legend of a Fallen City', *Eye to I* (Malta: Said International Ltd, 1994), pp 15–16.

ORIGINS AND INFLUENCES

Architecture can only be sustained today as a critical practice if it assumes an arrière-garde *position, that is to say, one which distances itself equally from the Enlightenment myth of progress and from a reactionary, unrealistic impulse to return to the architectonic forms of the pre-industrial past.*[1]

In the 1983 essay from which this quote was taken, Kenneth Frampton set out the notion of Critical Regionalism. In doing so, however, he was building on the work of earlier pioneers, as were the architects whose work he championed: Bernard Rudofsky, Geoffrey Bawa, Aris Konstantinidis, Hassan Fathy and a host of others who came before him and advocated a reassessment of Modernism that took into account local conditions. From Malta's past and its position as a meeting place of cultures, Richard England derived an architecture which blends the traditions and languages of southern Europe and the Middle East. From the Baroque churches of the Mediterranean (so much a part of Malta's landscape) he developed a love of sensuous forms, and from the Arabs he learnt a language of shade and simplicity, of cool courtyards and cubic houses.

The architects and theorists who have since been grouped in the new category of Critical Regionalism tended to have more success in the Mediterranean, where the vernacular was already broadly in line with an accepted way of working. From Carlo Scarpa to Alvaro Siza and even the harsh, seemingly international modern forms of Sert and Coderch, the postwar avant-garde in the Mediterranean had always taken into account the meanings and referential framework of history.

Richard England fits into this category along with architects as diverse as Imre Makovecz in Hungary and Abdel El Wakil in Egypt. But, in respect of the development of the regional, Mediterranean consciousness, the influence of one figure in particular is useful in illuminating and understanding the work of England himself. Italian architect and designer Gio Ponti's ideas and designs grew out of a coherent vein of Italian Modernism which had always appreciated the legacy of history and which often had no desire to stand out, to blast away the past and start again in a deliberately iconoclastic manner, as did the Modernism of many of his European contemporaries. England writes:

> He believed that the dogmatic imperatives of the International Style, accompanied by their declamatory revolutionary dialogues, had resulted in a loss of spiritual qualities, and that an approach towards an architecture capable of producing a 'lessening of unhappiness' could remedy this and reintroduce the much needed 'emotional' aspect to contemporary built environments.

In his architectural philosophy he remained incontestably humanistic and his buildings essentially glorify and respect both their users and on-lookers … The extraordinary versatility shown in the wide variety of his long-lasting activities was not surprising as this multi-disciplinary approach forms part of the grand tradition of the ancient masters of his land. Gio Ponti's buildings, in the most difficult period of modern architecture, rose from the stolid facelessness of modern rationalism to pulsate on an elevated plane of poetry. For this, his place in history is secure.[2]

Ponti had visited Malta in 1960 and, after an introduction engineered by his father, England was invited to go to Milan to work in Ponti's studio. The architect still talks of the profound influence this period had on him. Ponti, with his editorship of *Domus*, his designs for furniture, ceramics, costumes, glass, fabrics and almost anything else, was almost single-handedly responsible for setting up Milan as the world's capital of design. He was as close as the twentieth century came to a Renaissance man. Ponti's vigour and enthusiasm for all the fields of culture and his refusal to set limits on the range of his involvement in the arts appear to have deeply affected his Maltese amanuensis, as England has turned his hand to everything from sculpture to stamp design, from stage sets to volumes of poetry.

While Ponti's appearance on the Maltese scene was fleeting, out of all proportion to his influence on the subject of this book, when looking at England's formative influences mention is also required of two figures who spent a great deal of time on an island which came to enchant them. The first of these was Sir Basil Spence, the second Victor Pasmore.

Spence has come to be seen as the architect who brought the formal invention of the two quintessential English architects, Wren and Lutyens (in whose office he began his career), into the twentieth century. His best-known and most praised work, Coventry Cathedral, is described by England as 'a most inspiring and spiritual experience'.[3] He continues: 'Within its walls, Spence was able to successfully integrate the work of such artists as Sutherland, Piper and Epstein with his architecture. The resultant total ambience which amalgamates the bombed ruins of the original Cathedral building is one which is impregnated with both religious solemnity and a deep sense of liturgical ritual'.[4] Coventry Cathedral was not, however, a work of the avant-garde. Its conservative tectonic form and layout were a world away from the liturgical modern of Gottfried Böhm or Rudolf Schwarz. What is remarkable about Coventry, though, is that Spence managed to reconcile modern and historical architectural form, to create a genuinely popular architectural work (popular with the public at least, if not always the critics). In this, the cathedral, as well as Spence's other, more radical and sculptural schemes, certainly and visibly influenced the work of Richard England. Although it is for the cathedral that Spence became known, other of his schemes, particularly the brilliant designs for Sussex University and the British Embassy building in Rome, were similarly influential on the young Maltese architect. Spence's sculptural approach, his urbane massing and an eye which sprang essentially from his experiences in Lutyens' office and the Arts and Crafts sensibility of humane building, remain a powerful inspiration.

Spence acquired a farmhouse in Fawwara in Malta and spent a long period remodelling it with additions including a pool 'scooped out of the local rock face' and a 'mono-cellular space perched on the cliff-top which he used as a studio'.[5] England writes: 'Here, on many an occasion, one could watch Spence at work, both at the painting easel and also at the drawing board. The remarkable dexterity of his graphic skill was sure to impress any onlooker'.[6] Spence's sculptural approach and carefully massed composition, although it has never been universally popular, has nevertheless exerted a powerful influence on the generations that followed him. England has attributed Spence's un-English preoccupation with (and sensitive handling of) light and shadow to his upbringing in India. It is certainly noticeable in England's work, although there is little superficial similarity in the architects' work, England's *oeuvre* being so obviously Mediterranean. In an obituary England wrote that he had come to regard Spence as a father figure once his own father had died. There could be no greater revelation of the effect Spence had on England as not only an architect but an individual.

English artist Victor Pasmore was also a major formative influence on the life and work of Richard England, and another key figure in the erratic history of British Modernism. Like Spence, Pasmore became enchanted with Malta and, buying a farmhouse there, made it his home. He was a late convert to abstraction, only truly embracing it after the end of the Second World War. His earlier work had been characterised by exquisite and subtle landscapes. However, once he turned to abstraction he leapt into it and pushed British art forward through teaching and sculpture. He was among the few artists to cross over the often-blurred line between architecture and fine art. His public sculpture, or rather pavilion, in Peterlee New Town (a town which he had also been instrumental in planning), completed in 1970 although now poorly maintained, was a masterly play of concrete volumes. Heavily vandalised and reconfigured soon after

Top: Traditional Maltese townscape with a water cistern in the foreground. A Baroque church dominates limestone cube structures

Bottom: Limestone quarry face, Malta

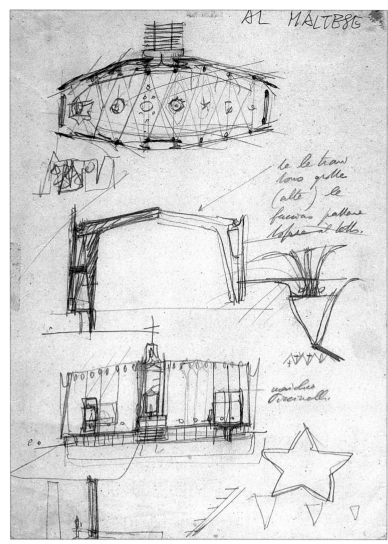

Top: Gio Ponti concept sketch for the church of San Carlo Hospital, Milan, Italy, with a note addressed to Richard England: *'Al Maltese'*

Bottom: Sir Basil Spence drawing for the British Embassy in Rome

Right: Victor Pasmore signing mural in A Garden for Myriam, 1998

its completion, it has been a controversial monument. Yet it has been misportrayed as an unpopular one. Pasmore was apparently delighted that local kids had been smoking and hiding away in the sculpture's recesses and he was not at all offended, rather he was happy with the engagement of local graffiti artists. This generous attitude towards art in the public realm was odd for Britain and is a fine example of how radical Pasmore actually was – an artist absolutely not precious about his work. Pasmore's final work of art was a mural etched in marble adjacent to Richard England's garden pool.

England writes of Pasmore:

In 1966, he acquired a farmhouse in Malta and, although his painting became more colourful, intense and free-flowing, he constantly denied that the Malta light, land and seascapes had any effect on his art. Within the high walls of this ethnic building through a series of highly individual interventions, he created an environmental totality, synthesizing painting and sculpture; a form of Mediterranean re-interpretation of his pavilion at Peterlee. The basic architectural forms of the island's vernacular architecture, basking under the strong Malta sun, were forms which Pasmore related and took to easily, as his formal geometry of the relief works of the late 50s and early 60s indicate. With his unerring eye, he superimposed elements and meandering lines to create a fascinating combination of various expression of the visual arts. The numerous walled enclosures of this solitary farmhouse, adjacent to the village of Gudja, remain an impressive testament to Pasmore's sophisticated expression of simplicity performed within tight restricted parameters, leaving little or no margin for error. The swimming pool area, with its various points embarking on long meandering walks forming lines journeying from wall to floor to under-water surface, provides a sublime artistic expression in three dimensional form ... Pasmore's constant research for the elimination of the non-essential, together with his frequent conversations relating to arguments about such themes as science and religion; sacred and profane; emotion and intellect; freedom and logic and other such ambivalent paradoxes were always not only a great influence, but also a valuable guiding set of artistic parameters.[7]

England was also responsible for Pasmore's only public commission in Malta, a freestanding mural at the Central Bank of Malta building within the St James Counterguard walls (see page 101). The two parts of this single work embodied exactly those paradoxes of which England wrote, and were entitled 'Faith and Reason' and 'Science and Faith'.

The grouping of Ponti, Spence and Pasmore may seem odd, but they also make up a remarkable cross section of twentieth-century art and design. The two British figures, Spence and Pasmore, are here through providence, through their serendipitous association with Malta and their ensuing relationship with Richard England. However it is Ponti, perhaps, whose professional influence made the deepest impression on England's architecture. Although the broader Italian architectural scene of the 1960s exerted a profound influence on England (with figures of the stature of Ernesto Rogers, Franco Albini and Carlo Scarpa all playing important roles), it was Ponti's broad base as a designer and his wide-ranging interest in the arts that particularly inspired the work of his former pupil.

For Ponti, there was little distinction between the arts, between building and design, writing, painting, pottery and so on. He was also among the first to identify a Mediterranean way of building and to propose a continuity with that vernacular – a self-effacing modernisation of Mediterranean archetype. He once wrote that: 'The Mediterranean taught Rudofksy and Rudofsky taught me.'[8] His was an architecture that acknowledged its precedents, the civilisations that preceded it, and led inexorably towards it. The influence of his words can be felt in all England's buildings:

The Mediterranean is large, and its shores along the coasts of Morocco, Spain, France, Sardinia, Sicily, Italy and the Tyrrhenian and the Adriatic, Greece, Anatolia, Palestine, Egypt, Libya, Tunisia and Algeria have washed over many different histories, civilisations, and climates, so much so that a peremptory definition of Mediterranean architecture that does not lend itself to discussion and stylistic correction cannot be given ... It is, however, a fact that such an architecture exists, that walls exist that wed themselves to Mediterranean pines and palms, to the skies, the sun and the waves of the Mediterranean ... The identification of this general character and the art of using it to build is essential for us, since our shores, blessed by a happy sun, should exert an attraction that corresponds to evident national interests. This function of attracting should progress with two aims: to preserve the character, beauty, and nobility of our shores, and to enhance them with our constructions.[9]

Notes

1. Hal Foster (ed), *The Anti Aesthetic* (Washington, DC: Bay Press), p 20.
2. Murial Emanuel (ed), *Contemporary Architects* (London: St James Press, 1994), p 762.
3. Petra Bianchi and Peter Serracino Inglott (eds), *Encounters with Malta* (Malta: Encounter Books, 2000), p 328.
4. *Ibid*, p 328.
5. *Ibid*, p 329.
6. *Ibid*, p 329.
7. *Ibid*, p 333.
8. Lisa Licitra Ponti, *Gio Ponti, The Complete Work 1923–1978* (London: Thames and Hudson, 1990), p 96.
9. Ugo La Pietra, *Gio Ponti* (New York: Rizzoli, 1996), p 100.

EARLY WORKS

Modern architecture hit Malta hard. And it was not always the best type. Malta's greatest period of expansion since Valletta was built by the knights in the sixteenth century, was the 1960s, prompted by the boom in tourism. This vast, almost untrammelled expansion unfortunately coincided with one of the bleakest moments in the history of architecture. Malta suffered, as did most of the Mediterranean. It was during this period that Richard England launched his career.

It would be easy, though not entirely untrue, to say that in this morass of lowest-common-denominator tourist Modernism, it was not difficult for a good architect to make a mark and to stand out. But England's best works of this remarkably prolific and fecund period incorporated elements of the local vernacular and of the European avant-garde which have ensured that those of his works that have survived are worthy of examination. In *Connections: the Architecture of Richard England 1964–84*, Dennis Sharp wrote:

> Richard England's early buildings put his own very distinctive stamp of Mediterranean modernism on the holiday hotel scene. These buildings also reflect his continuing interest in the local vernacular style of the island. He has always been concerned with an architecture that is distinctive in its form as well as relating it to a continuity of existing building traditions. This combination results in the architecture being able to give a sense of meaning to a 'place' – an argument which is essential to England's thinking.[1]

In the Ramla Bay Hotel, Marfa (1964), the influences of Le Corbusier (particularly his Maisons Jaoul) and, perhaps in its volumes, the legacy of Louis Kahn, become visible, while in the vaulted *brises-soleil* of the Paradise Bay Hotel (1963) they were even clearer. The clean Modernist lines of the Joinwell showrooms in Sliema (also 1964) however, are indicative of the search for a purer, more urbane (and more international) Modernism. This little building, with its clearly expressed concrete structural elements and its slatted upper storeys, stands out from its neighbours in this downtown shopping district as a pure structure of great clarity which has not dated at all. The Dolphin Court apartment building at Ta'Xbiex (1964) presents a more abstract, painterly elevation in which the bold horizontals of the balconies create an abstract work juxtaposed with the by now familiar arches and white walls of the structure.

The Villa La Maltija (1966) at San Pawl tat-Targa is a complex composition in which each element of the plan, each space, is expressed separately on the elevations. The rounded corners recall the walls of Manikata while the massing displays England's characteristic method of viewing each building as a city in microcosm with a carefully considered distribution of elements and hierarchy of internal spaces. The expanses of blank wall, tiny openings and shadows caused by the protruding structural elements, however, evoke the traditional townscape of the Middle East and recall the exquisite reinterpretation of the Arab vernacular expressed in the domestic buildings of Hassan Fathy. Similar rounded elements reoccur in the Dolmen Hotel in Qawra (also 1966) where their verticality and staggered masses seem to have stemmed from the visionary, Futurist monuments of Antonio Sant'Elia and Mario Chiattone. The Festaval tourist village development in Mellieha Bay (1980) would return to Futurist concepts in a striking set of masonry terraces stepped into landscape, again reminiscent of the monumental urban visions of Sant'Elia but here combined with the rigorous planes of Takefumi Aida or Arata Isozaki.

If the details of the Dolmen Hotel seemed to owe something to the visions of Italian Futurists, then the Ta'Monita tourist village at Marsascala (1968), a series of terraces climbing up the side of a seaside hill, evokes the eerie, deserted, dream-like townscapes of the Surrealists. Other projects around the same time, including the Salina Bay Hotel (1970), the Computer Centre for the Mid-Med Bank, Qormi, the Tower Palace Hotel, Sliema (both 1968) and the much later Marina San Gorg apartments at St George's Bay (1981, now demolished) blend the now familiar elements of ochre stone or concrete and deep, recessed arcades and windows to create a consistent language of solid and void, dark and light, and a tectonic language rooted in local conditions and traditions. The arcades, arches and Mannerist touches also presaged the coming of Post-Modernism and the worldwide reinterpretation of classical and vernacular forms that would become more pronounced in the architect's later works.

Notes

1. Charles Knevitt, *Connections: the Architecture of Richard England 1964–84* (London: Lund Humphries, 1984), p 8.

Opposite top left: Paradise Bay Hotel, Marfa, Malta, 1963
Opposite top right: Ramla Bay Hotel, Marfa, Malta, 1964
Opposite bottom left: Joinwell showrooms, Sliema, Malta, 1964
Opposite bottom right: Dolphin Court apartments, Ta'Xbiex, 1964

ABOVE: Villa La Maltija, Naxxar, Malta, 1966. *Detail of masonry screen–wall*

RIGHT: Villa La Maltija, Naxxar. *Plan: 1 Entrance; 2 Hall; 3 Garage; 4 Bedrooms; 5 Living room; 6 Bar; 7 Dining; 8 Kitchen; 9 Service stairs; 10 Main stairs; 11 Maid's quarters; 12 Pantry; 13 Bridge; 14 Garden*

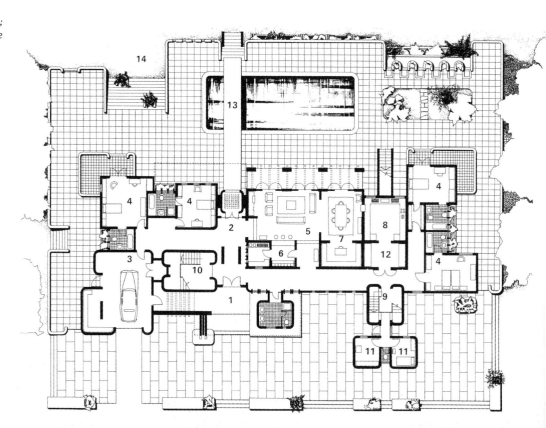

LEFT: Villa La Maltija, Naxxar. *Concept sketch*
BELOW: Villa La Maltija, Naxxar.

19 Early Works

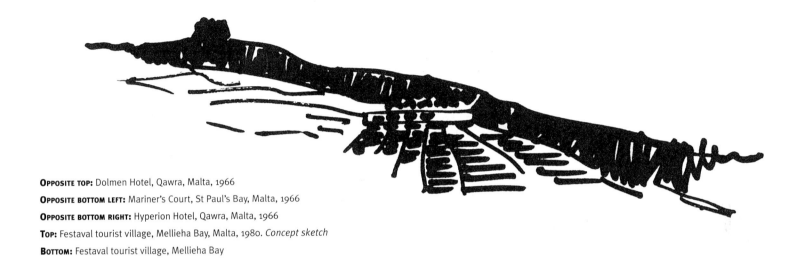

Opposite top: Dolmen Hotel, Qawra, Malta, 1966

Opposite bottom left: Mariner's Court, St Paul's Bay, Malta, 1966

Opposite bottom right: Hyperion Hotel, Qawra, Malta, 1966

Top: Festaval tourist village, Mellieha Bay, Malta, 1980. *Concept sketch*

Bottom: Festaval tourist village, Mellieha Bay

Richard England

Opposite: Cavalieri Hotel, St Julians, Malta, 1968

Top left: Ta'Monita tourist village, Marsascala, Malta, 1968

Top right: Mid-Med Bank Computer Centre, Qormi, Malta, 1968

Bottom left: Salina Bay Hotel, Salina Bay, Malta, 1970

Bottom right: Marina San Gorg apartments, St George's Bay, St Julians, Malta, 1981; demolished 1998

CHURCH OF ST JOSEPH, MANIKATA

The sacredness of space lies in its memories.[1]

If what England says is really so, then the church at Manikata reaches back to Malta's earliest memories of civilisation, the stone temples that form such an unforgettable part of the island's man-made landscape. Malta's megalithic temples at Hagar Qim, Mnajdra, Tarxien, Hal Saflieni and Ggantija are remarkable not only for their age (roughly 3600–2500 BC) but for their spatial complexity. Whereas Stonehenge, Avebury and the other ancient monuments of northern and western Europe tend towards simplistic stone circles or lines of menhirs or sarcens, the Maltese temples are characterised by their curvaceous, womb-like interior spaces and the progression through a series of carefully constructed chambers, usually axial, and occasionally introducing skews and diversions from the central axis.

If these temples are the archetypal sacred spaces of the island, living on in a collective unconscious as mysterious remnants of a great lost culture, then the island's *girnas* (rounded dry-stone walled huts) are their profane equivalent. These odd little structures stand like Martello towers in the rural Maltese landscape, yet their function is not more elevated than that of a tool shed. These traditional buildings are firmly rooted in Malta's vernacular tradition and their rocky, curvaceous form allows them to dwell in the landscape as naturally and comfortably as the boulders that scatter the region. The echoes of both the complex and intriguing temples and the prosaic vernacular sheds can be heard in the hill-top church of St Joseph in Manikata.

The silent, arid landscape in which the small church of St Joseph sits seems to be reflected in the building's ochre walls and the stony sculptures which surround it. The same combination of silent stones and the harsh, unforgiving sunshine so overwhelming at the temple sites is immediately apparent in Manikata. The building rises out of the rough stone landscape as if it were an outcrop or an object thrown up from the earth itself. The influence of the curving, feminine spaces of the temples is most clearly seen in the plan. The site is defined by a precinct bounded by a low wall framing a rectangle with broadly curving edges. The gravelled ground is dotted with boulders of local origin, giving the area the appearance of a kind of Zen garden, a space for the contemplation of the complexity of nature. The church itself is a composition of curving, battered planes pierced only by small openings, giving the impression of a massive, fortified structure recalling the forts and bunkers that litter the coastline of this much-besieged island.

The solid walls contain a space that is essentially a lozenge with a dislocation roughly at its centre. This fracture creates not only a route into the building but also defines a zone visually separating the nave from the sanctuary. I say visually separating to acknowledge one of the most important facets of this remarkable little building. Designed in 1962, the church presaged many of the fundamental changes brought about by the Second Vatican Council. In traditional churches the separation of clergy and laity had been one of the cornerstones of internal planning. Vatican II encouraged a revival of the Early Church plan in which celebrant and congregation form one body with the building – the separation is broken down to allow all to feel as one. This was an enormous change in ideology which led to a reassessment of the whole of church architecture the like of which had not been seen since the Gothic cathedrals. England's use of curving, embracing walls and a womb-like intimacy was pioneering and would prove highly influential in later church designs. But it also looks back to the ideas of pioneering Modernists like Rudolf Schwarz, whose book *The Church Incarnate* later proved a key text of liturgical renewal. In it he talked of his own ideas:

> The structure is simple, open roundedness … it is that roundedness which is end and shelter, the simple presence of joy, the awaiting light – that into which the people finally surrender themselves as if into an open hand.[2]

The two interlocking, dislocated parts of the plan at Manikata also allow for the ingenious entrance system whereby that fracture between the volumes makes for a break in the continuity of the walls (a kind of snail's shell effect) and creates an obvious entrance without the need for a formal gesture on the elevation to highlight it.

In his 1980 book *Manikata: the Making of a Church*, Charles Knevitt described the building lyrically:

> There are two main entrances to the church: one from the east, which catches the streaming early morning sun, the other from the west, shielded from the afternoon heat by a portico through which the sky and distant landscape can be seen when approached from either north or south. But the most direct route into the church is from the road which winds its circuitous way from Manikata village … From the south, two parallel flights of shallow steps, held apart by the muscular sweep of a wing wall … draw worshippers into the tight, dark funnel created by the broad, timber-relief doors and beside a rubble field-stone cross set into the wall. The dividing wall, with rectangular openings punched through it, acts as a buffer against the wind and as a *brise-soleil* beating off the scorching sun, providing cool cavernous shade while brilliant rhomboids of

Richard England

ABOVE: Church of St Joseph, Manikata. *Entrance porch*
BELOW: Church of St Joseph, Manikata. *Section*

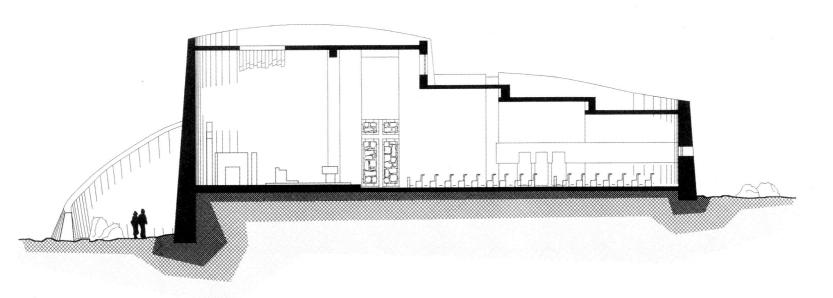

Opposite top: Church of St Joseph, Manikata. *City of Towers, concrete sculpture designed by Richard England, 1974*

Opposite bottom left: Church of St Joseph, Manikata. *East elevation*

Opposite bottom right: Church of St Joseph, Manikata. *Boulder garden and side entrance to the church*

Above: Church of St Joseph, Manikata. *View of the interior*

Left: Church of St Joseph, Manikata. *View of the sanctuary space, showing the monolithic altar, table, baptisimal font and lectern*

SACRED SPACES

Religious architecture is not a question of architecture, but one of religion.[1]

The words of England's early mentor, Gio Ponti, serve as a fine summation to Richard England's extensive explorations into the field of sacred space. It is impossible to fail to notice the depth of belief and faith in Malta. The islanders' passion for church building is evident in the smallest villages. It is remarkable, almost absurd, to see the colossal Church of St John the Baptist in the small village of Xewkija on Gozo, crowned with one of the largest domes in the world, begun in the 1950s in pure Baroque. It reminds you that the islands have not only one of the oldest Christian communities (having been converted by St Paul after his shipwreck in AD 60) but also one of the most devout. Yet, strolling around the fantastic remains of the haunting prehistoric temple sites on the islands, the visitor cannot help but be struck by the continuity in faith and in the dedication to building places of worship. In a recent essay, Paolo Portoghesi puts England's architecture into the context of this rich Maltese inheritance of sacral architecture:

> Richard England in his travels of discovery of sacred places appears as a worthy son of the mysterious island in which sacredness expresses itself in primordial forms without redundancy and without temporal connotations. This is achieved beyond the confines of time and space, and in the process indicating a close relationship with the divine and the innermost self of the individual being.[2]

This essay appears at the beginning of the small volume entitled *Sacri Luoghi* (Sacred Places, see Introduction, p 11), a compendium of sketches by the architect of churches and religious buildings from Mecca to Mexico which culminates in a series of design sketches for his own works in Malta. Beginning with the Manikata church this small but rich journey through a plethora of sacred buildings is perhaps the finest summation of England's ongoing fascination with churches and chapels. From the tiny private chapels to the Church of St Francis of Assisi, Qawra, and the theatrical stands for two papal visits to Malta, these finely wrought sketches express the search for the balance between darkness and light, between solid and space, and between the realms of the interior and the urban, the sacred and the profane.

Undoubtedly England's most important sacred building remains the church of Manikata, a building which proved critical in the evolution of new ideas on not only sacred space in the wake of Vatican II but also in the development of notions of the relationship of modern architecture to place and climate, to history, archetype and the local subconscious. This is why this particular building has been lifted out to form a chapter on its own.

Post-Manikata, England's architecture has often been stagey and theatrical, adorned with multiple layers and screens to give depth to often small buildings, but he is always careful to ensure that his churches and sacred spaces are not mere gestures. In addressing the fundamental reforms of Vatican II, the Church's profound reassessment of the nature of the liturgy and consequently of the architecture of churches, England writes:

> The church of the Third Millennium must therefore primarily read as a place of welcome and convocation. The new prayer spaces are not to be conceived as houses of God; nor as some pre-echo of heaven, but more tangibly as places of convergence and dialogue between God and man ... The contemporary church must ultimately be seen as a locus where sacred time and sacred space are brought together to evoke the ritual of eternal presence.[3]

In understanding England's recent church and chapel buildings, this notion of the church as meeting place is paramount yet always tempered by the architect's seemingly paradoxical quest for contemplative space. In the same way that one can stand in a piazza, surrounded by crowds and by the throng of life, yet feel either oppressed by the crowd or embraced by it, either alienated or alive to the rhythm of the city, the architect has to reconcile the meditative with the public. The chapel at Dar il-Hanin Samaritan becomes an extension of the urbane piazza which sits at the heart of this communal development. Light and airy, with extensively glazed walls, the interior is only anchored to the ground by a heavy stone altar – this is sacred space as public place.

The Millennium Chapel in Paceville, Malta's throbbing nightlife district, perfectly illustrates the resolution of this paradox. The building was conceived as a place of refuge and contemplation for the international and home-grown clubbers descending on the area in droves. The embrace of its quiet, subdued space provides an antidote to the teeming streets and the perennial cliché of the loneliest place being a crowd. It seems that this dark little interior is always inhabited – the need for this kind of escape is obviously there. The gridded end wall of the worship space is dotted with halogen lights to evoke a starry sky, at the centre of which is a slender wooden cross framed by a pair of local, unhewn rocks – the earth and the heavens represented together – the empty cross (signifying a resurrected rather than a suffering, earthbound Christ) as the symbol which unites them. Because of the constant, quiet stream of visitors, and although it allows for quiet contemplation in the presence of the

OPPOSITE: Church of St Francis of Assisi, Qawra, Malta, 1988–98. *External view*

evoke the architecture of the Middle East. The second mausoleum is composed of more angular forms creating a spiky roofscape that contrasts strongly with the dark, shadowy forms of the cypresses that inhabit the cemetery. The third of the mausolea is more spatially complex, its interior space open to the sky forming a kind of courtyard behind containing walls, within which can be glimpsed an arrangement of rough boulders. A standing cross casts a deep shadow across the walls. In all three structures, England's urban approach to building form is made manifest – each mausoleum seems to represent an attempt to create a small slice of urban architecture, thereby reinforcing the notion of the cemetery as a city of the dead, an ordered collection of the villas of memory.

This approach, however, has not been limited to these chapels of repose: it is a strain which runs throughout the architect's work and which, even in the tiniest of spaces, becomes a governing, ordering idea. The now demolished Chapel of St Andrew in Pembroke represented another example of the approach seen also in England's gardens. The chapel, which was originally built by German prisoners of war on the island and later served British soldiers garrisoned there, had fallen into disrepair after their departure in 1979. When the barracks were replaced by housing, the church became necessary once more and England was commissioned to restore and expand the existing structure. In an attempt to knit the building into the new fabric, the architect created a piazza as a boundary zone between the sacred space and the streets that surrounded it. Using a simple, platonic vocabulary of forms including pyramids, columns, crosses and cubes, as well as arcades and isolated fragments of walls, England made an urbane space that functioned as both public square and garden of contemplation. In its rich colours (terracotta, sky blue, pink and lilac), this garden echoed the vibrancy of Barragán's gardens. The church itself was given a sky-blue screen facade, punched through with a rose window and bell openings which opened only on to the sky itself. Its interior was composed in a similarly urbane fashion. Behind the screen a new columnated internal narthex was created to extend the processional way which begins in the garden of tectonic elements and which sets up the formal, axial orientation of the building. The forms inhabiting the sanctuary included a cylindrical lectern, columnated screen and the blocky altar carved of a single pike of stone which England has made a trademark. As at the meditation chapel at Naxxar, the ceiling above the altar descends in a series of corbelled steps to the east wall, a nod to the notion of a path to the vaults of heaven.

The crypt of the Blessed Gorg Preca Church at Blata I-Bajda, a structure built to house the remains of the eponymous holy man (within an existing church of 1958) presented the opportunity to combine the architecture of death with space for worship in a way which has seldom been presented to architects in recent years. The insertion of a vaulted crypt space into an impressive cylindrical

Opposite top: Mortuary chapel, Addolorata Cemetery, Paola, Malta, 1998. *Concept skech*
Opposite bottom left: Addolorata Cemetery, Paola, 1979. *Chapel G*
Opposite bottom right: Addolorata Cemetery, Paola, 1975. *Chapel B*
Above: Addolorata Cemetery, Paola, 1998. *Chapel E.T.*

ABOVE: Chapel of St Andrew, Pembroke, Malta, 1988; demolished 1999. *View of the entrance garden*

OPPOSITE: Chapel of St Andrew, Pembroke. *View of the sanctuary area*

OPPOSITE: Blessed Gorg Preca crypt, Blata I-Bajda, Malta, 2001. *Concept sketch*

FAR LEFT: Blessed Gorg Preca crypt, Blata I-Bajda

LEFT: Blessed Gorg Preca crypt, Blata I-Bajda. *Detail of altar walls*

BELOW: Blessed Gorg Preca crypt, Blata I-Bajda. *Chapel of the Blessed Sacrament*

Millennium Chapel, Paceville, Malta, 1999

IL TEATRO DELL'ARCHITETTURA –
WATERS OF REFLECTION

The ancients built Valdrada on the shores of a lake ...Thus the traveller, arriving, sees two cities: one erected above the lake, and the other reflected, upside-down. Nothing exists or happens in the one Valdrada that the other Valdrada does not repeat, because the city was so constructed that its every point would be reflected in its mirror, and the Valdrada down in the water contains not only all the flutings and juttings of the facades ... but also the rooms' interiors with ceilings and floors, the perspective of the halls, the mirrors of the wardrobes.[1]

Italo Calvino's paean to the inscrutable and infinite beauty (and terror) of Venice is also one of the most lyrical testaments to the relationship of water to architecture. In Calvino's world the water creates a mirror in which the reflection becomes as real, or more real, than reality. There is more than a hint of Narcissus and a wry dig at the enthralment of the superficial for which La Serenissima has often been criticised. Yet the juxtaposition of water and buildings can create an almost mesmeric atmosphere. The way buildings are reflected in the waters is so often the way cities are defined. Whether it is the magnificent view of Istanbul and the minarets and domes of its mosques approaching from the Bosphorus, the reflection of the spires of Notre Dame in the Seine or of the Castel Sant' Angelo in the Tiber, the waterways and seas around cities both define their character and reflect the light and darkness that emanate from their structures and streets.

The cities of Malta are as defined by the sea as any cities in Europe. A tiny island with a harsh, dry climate, water is always on the agenda in Malta. In Valletta in particular the ideal Renaissance grid plan assures that there is always a view of the glinting sea down any narrow street – one is always made aware of the importance of the Mediterranean. While from the sea the capacious domes of the island's capital dominate the skyline. A city's relationship with the sea is never accidental: the city has grown there because of the waterway, never vice versa. The sea becomes, in effect, a kind of audience to the city's beauty, or at least comparable to the seats in an amphitheatre which surrounds a stage, the vehicle for an audience who needs to be impressed or, in the case of potential invaders, deterred from arriving on boats from afar. Whether in Venice, Istanbul, Stockholm or New York, the defining image is of arrival via sea. The silhouette of spires, minarets or skyscrapers is far more a stage set than a practical agglomeration of masses. Bearing the theatricality of this kind of urbanism in mind, this section embraces works based around water in a microcosm of the island's eternal relationship with the sea, but also includes works for the theatre and works of spectacle – buildings designed to house an audience.

In the Aquasun Lido, St Julians (1983), England combined stage-set theatricality with the addressing of water. Blending elements of the Post-Modern (then at its intellectual and theoretical zenith) with glimpses of Pop Art and Neo-Rationalism, this was a truly Mediterranean stage-set architecture – the theatre brought to the poolside. In *Connections: the Architecture of Richard England 1964–84*, Charles Knevitt writes:

> Recalling the dreamlike world of De Chirico, Aquasun Lido is a place conceived as an illusory stage to release the frozen memories of one's childhood, to summon the lost laughter of youth, a Surrealist space which rehabilitates superstition and magic.[2]

Those using the pool and its surroundings become both actors and audience in an enthralling piece of architectural theatre as influential (but more subtle) in its reinterpretation of classical urban Mediterranean form as Charles Moore's more elaborate Piazza d'Italia in New Orleans (completed in 1979). England writes:

> The Aquasun Lido architecture seeks an expression which invites participation of its users on many levels and provides a form of stepping stone or threshold for man to walk through into a specific area of relaxation and recuperation. An area built and orchestrated in childhood game-images, yet belonging to the concrete tangible reality of the world today. Its forms and layout also evoke the intimacies and social functionalism of traditional Mediterranean village squares. It is, above all, a creation based on a series of deeper recollective images which work to free frozen memories of one's lost dreams of childhood. This is an architecture of primal imagery, drawing its roots and inspiration from basic house-temple prototypes and in its layers of quintessence its forms relate to the evolution of the making of architecture. The geometric relationships of its archetypal forms relate to those origins of architecture in their earliest evolutionary forms. The basic building prototype of Primitive Hut evolving to Ideal Temple emerges in the order, hierarchy and sequential spaces of this place. These are

Aquasun Lido, St Julians, Malta, 1983

images, instantly recognisable features, which not only relate to the origins of man's first established forms as a builder, but which function on our psyche to recollect individual 'remembered things' from childhood, for as Gaston Bachelard has taught us, it is the child in man that holds the essential key to our whole existence.[3]

In A Garden for Myriam, built a year earlier for the architect's wife at their home, England played with the same urban and archetypal Mediterranean forms to create a complex and intriguingly theatrical series of architectural set pieces. Returning once more to Charles Knevitt's poetic description:

> Two principal axes generate the dynamics of the garden: one from the rear of the house, the other from an Ikebana studio dating from 1966, which intersect at the pool. Cosmic symbols from a Metaphysical world are placed around it: cyclical time is represented by the zodiacal twelve windows of a Memory Wall, its layers overlapping and interpenetrating; the black void of the Arch of Amnesia threatens emptiness or oblivion. The Staircase of Desire leads from the terrestrial to

the celestial; The Sentinels of Time and Space evoke in miniature the calendar stones of pre-history; while the Steps of Sagacity, a simple equilateral pediment on a single, central column recalls the traditional ridge-pole of Shinto buildings. Man here is the observer of a different world, as composer of his own allegorical space, where a dozen features crave his attention and perception.[4]

The purpose of the garden is described by England in his *In Search of Silent Spaces* as an 'idealistic precinct, laid out to provide occasional glimpses of rare terrestrial paradisal patches – a paradigm of peace whose rhythms serve to calm, soothe and focus on the serene. A space designed as a private Arcadia, concerned predominantly with the users' personal journeys and recollections in time'.[5] This also has much to do with the architect's preoccupations with silence and with a kind of English Romantic notion of folly and melancholy. England writes:

> This garden is a space woven in threads of SILENCE to enable us to rediscover in today's terms the usefulness of the useless. It is an environment of crystalline limpidity, steeped in

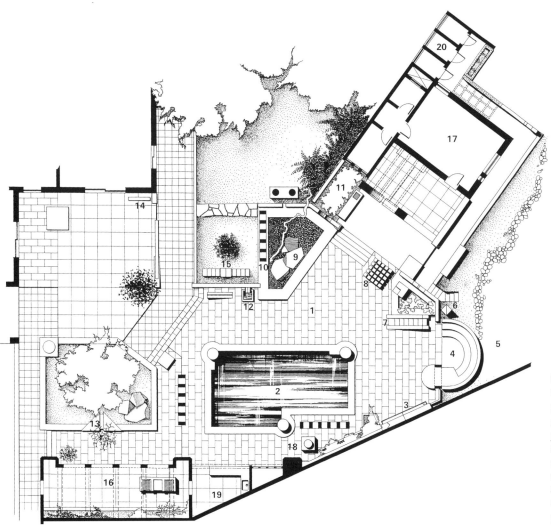

OPPOSITE: A Garden for Myriam, St Julians, Malta, 1982. *Night view of pool area*

LEFT: A Garden for Myriam, St Julians. *Plan: 1 Theatre of Memory; 2 Waters of Reflection; 3 Memory wall; 4 Temenos; 5 Secret Garden; 6 Pinnacle of Peace; 7 Staircase of Desire; 8 Sentinels of Space and Time; 9 Garden of Quintessence; 10 Cloister of Remembrance; 11 Scented Garden; 12 Fountain of Laments; 13 Pyramid of Transcendence; 14 Memory Screen; 15 Steps of Sagacity; 16 Hermitage of Solitude; 17 Ikebana Studio; 18 Goddess of Youth; 19 Bar; 20 Toilets*

BELOW: A Garden for Myriam, St Julians

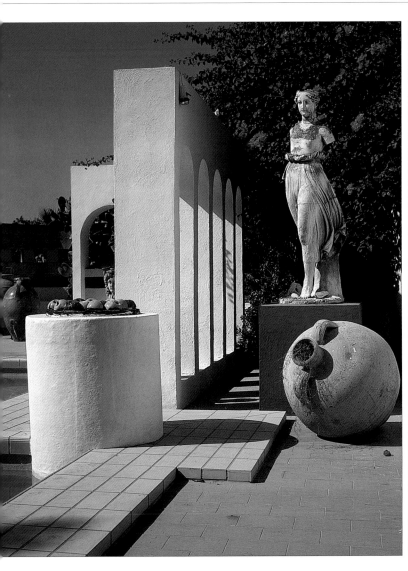

ABOVE: Ir-Razzett ta' Sandrina, Mgarr, Malta, 1988–93. *Staircase to pool area*
OPPOSITE TOP: Ir-Razzett ta' Sandrina, Mgarr. *Plan*
OPPOSITE BOTTOM: Ir-Razzett ta' Sandrina, Mgarr

overtones of nostalgia, conceived in the undulating candescent moods of a Mahler adagio.[6]

Although some of the same architectural themes (time, space, silence, memory, the Garden of Paradise) are explored in Ir-Razzett ta' Sandrina (1988–93), this is a simpler, more contemplative composition, where again the influence of two twentieth century greats – De Chirico and Barragán – is obvious. The latter of these once famously said: 'I believe that architects should design gardens to be used, as much as the houses they build, to develop a sense of beauty and the taste and inclination toward the fine arts and other spiritual values.'[7] In the garden of this converted farmhouse in northern Malta, as series of arcades and steps become both frames and screens for the landscape and the architecture itself, a wall, punched through with a row of square openings, terminates the pool and provides glimpses through to the harsh surrounding landscape and the horizon. The architectural interventions have the quiet emptiness of a De Chirico townscape, but the rich hues of blue and the piercing Maltese sunlight ensure that Barragán's influence is always there to temper the disturbing Surrealism with its Latin humanity. The legacy of the great Mexican architect again becomes apparent in the exquisite little chapel within the house where solid planes of colour, a stripped-down block of an altar and Zen garden gravel create a space that is part Malevich Suprematism and part Barragán grotto.

The colours of Barragán and the complexity and symbolism of form explored in the Garden for Myriam come together in a private villa in Siggiewi (1994). A crowded composition of urban elements creates a microcosmic townscape in a single building. Again the pool modulates the structure through reflection and through light. The intensity of its glinting blue reflects and refracts the blue of the sky, while the stone and the terracotta red of the structure echo the colours of the dry earth. Again, the tectonic language is of screens, arcades and platonic solids so that there is the constant illusion of depth and layering, as theatrical as England gets yet using a restrained collection of forms. The theatricality is not in decoration or in camp overplaying but in the density and intensity of the composition.

There is a building-block, toy-like quality to the architecture here, as in the Garden for Myriam, which accentuates the sense of the unreal, the otherworldly. A constant play of scale is meant to blur the boundaries between foreground and background, sculpture and architecture, cipher and reality. The laconic sense of emptiness and nagging discomfort we feel when looking at a De Chirico is combined with the same sense, when looking at that artist's work, of something else going on that we don't fully understand – beyond the frame or outside the scope of the picture – or of a sense of longing. It is this sense that keeps the work of the Surrealists and of Richard England so fresh and so consistently intriguing.

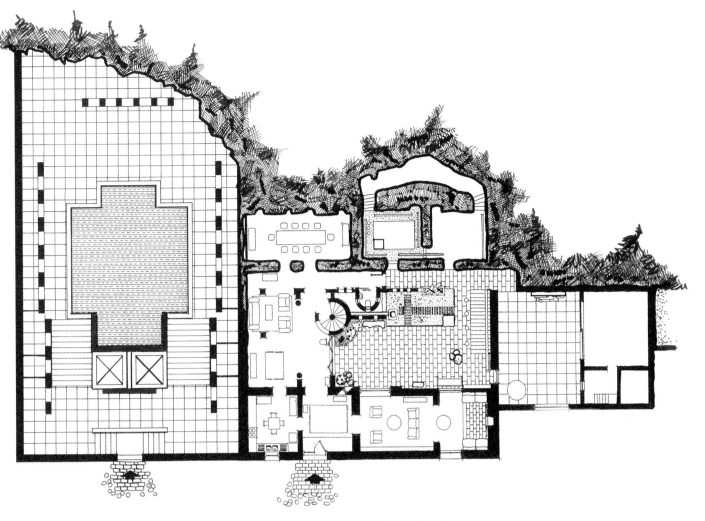

Right: Ir-Razzett ta' Sandrina, Mgarr. *Arched screen-wall in courtyard*
Below left: Ir-Razzett ta' Sandrina, Mgarr. *Concept sketch of swimming pool*
Below right: Ir-Razzett ta' Sandrina, Mgarr. *Swimming pool screen-wall*

Richard England

Ir-Razzett ta' Sandrina, Mgarr. *Courtyard with top-lit staircase tower*

England uses the same motifs of layering, of screens and of the recurring, stripped-down and abstracted language of Maltese architecture in more directly theatrical designs, for the stage itself. For a production of *Le Pescatrici* (a newly discovered opera by Haydn with a libretto by Goldoni), the simple white facades of Mediterranean houses tumble and skew across the stage while the twin-towered church dominates the background. In the sets for *The Maltese Cross* (Camilleri and Serracino Inglott) we see the recurrence of the haunting punched screen, this time without the consolation of the Maltese landscape being visible through its apertures, merely a grim blackness making it more akin to Rossi's Columbarium at San Cataldo, the central building of a city of the dead.

The relationship between theatre and sacred space is a close and natural one. The liturgy itself is a re-enactment of the Last Supper and of Christ's sacrifice, and the congregation's spectatorship and involvement in the mass is pure theatre. In fact the roots of post-classical theatre lie in the mystery plays which took place in the streets around the churches and cathedrals of medieval cities. This kind of religious theatre, a bible for the illiterate, was set up not in a separate designated space but in the very fabric of the city. In a series of theatrical designs for stands to accommodate individual gatherings and large audiences on the pope's visits to the island of Malta, England has created modern-day settings for exactly this kind of event. For the 1990 visit, England built stands at Floriana, Ta'Qali

and Mellieha. The latter two share a Baroque theme derived from the facades of the island's churches, while the former is a more geometric composition with a space-frame *brise-soleil* forming a canopy above it. The stand at Ta'Qali stadium was a more operatic affair, two grand stairs descending into an arena, their lines focusing on the pontiff's cathedra. For the visit in 2001, England built a stand at Floriana. Here, a great floating canopy echoed the bright yellow, curving and embracing form of a wall behind the pope's position. The canopy was supported on a pair of columns out of which grew a series of supports, the effect like a hi-tech memory of a pair of trees.

Just as he did in the Aquasun Lido and the various garden designs, England was concerned to create an urbane architecture out of the simplest of elements. The result is a series of minicities, urban forms created out of thin air and destined to return to the earth after a few short days, like fragments of a city appearing in a mirage.

Notes
1. Italo Calvino, *Invisible Cities* (London: Picador, 1979), pp 43–4.
2. Charles Knevitt, *Connections: the Architecture of Richard England 1964–84* (London: Lund Humphries, 1984), p 165.
3. Richard England, *Forms Borrowed from the Summer of My Childhood* (Tokyo: A+ U Publishing Co, 10, 1984) p 80.
4. Knevitt, *op cit*, p 155.
5. Richard England, *In Search of Silent Spaces* (Malta: MRSM Publications, 1983).
6. *Ibid.*
7. Charles Knevitt (ed), *Perspectives* (London: Lund Humphries, 1986), p 405.

Opposite: Private villa, Siggiewi, Malta, 1994. *View of garden and pool*

Below: Papal stand, Floriana, Malta, 2001

"LE PESPETTIVE"

Opposite top: *Le Pescatrici*, (music Joseph Haydn, libretto Goldoni), Manoel Theatre, Valletta, Malta, 2000. *Concept sketch*

Opposite bottom: *Le Pescatrici. Concept sketch*

Above: *Le Pescatrici. View of the stage*

Left: *The Maltese Cross*, (music Charles Camilleri, libretto Peter Serracino Inglott), Manoel Theatre, Valletta, Malta, 1995. *Concept sketch*

Castle of Happiness, 1999. *Concept sketch*

LEFT: Castle of Happiness, 1986

BELOW: *Compostella*, 1994, (music Charles Camilleri, libretto Peter Serracino Inglott), Manoel Theatre, Valletta, Malta. *Concept sketch*

URBAN SCHEMES – THE SILENCE IN BETWEEN

Richard England

In the conclusion to his monumental *The City in History*, Lewis Mumford wrote that:

> The final mission of the city is to further man's conscious participation in the cosmic and the historic process. Through its own complex and enduring structure, the city vastly augments man's ability to interpret these processes and take an active, formative part in them, so that every phase of the drama it stages shall have, to the highest degree possible, the illumination of consciousness, the stamp of purpose, the colour of love. That magnification of all the dimensions of life, through emotional communion, rational communication, technological mastery, and above all, dramatic representation, has been the supreme office of the city in history.[1]

Mumford's emphasis on the theatrical, the dramatic, is important. The city has always been about show as well as function. Edmund Bacon in *The Design of Cities* also makes the point that: 'One of the functions of architecture is the creation of spaces to intensify the drama of existence.'[2] To live in a city is to be on display, and to build in a city is to self-consciously leave a mark. Then there is the idea, always so attractive to architects, of building the city itself. Artists and architects from Leonardo (whose ideas profoundly influenced the idealised plan of Valletta) to Le Corbusier dreamed of creating whole cities in their singular visions. But there is also a stage in between these two poles, between the intervention into an existing urban fabric and the creation of a whole new metropolis. That is, a fragment of a city which is a microcosm of the larger organism (I say organism because, as Peter Ackroyd points out in his book *London: A Biography*, the city is as alive and responsive to stimuli as any animal [3]).

Most of Richard England's schemes are urban in some way. Even the secluded, dusty precincts of the Manikata church have the feel of a deserted city square, a space which was once at the heart of things but which has faded, like the ruins of great classical cities, into obscurity and isolation. His houses too are usually conceived as minicities, collections of fragments of urban townscape reduced in scale to allow a more expansive use of space and imagination. However, the three schemes grouped together here – Dar il-Hanin Samaritan, the University of Malta and Bab-al-Sheikh in Baghdad – have in common an urban approach: each is designed as a collection of buildings arranged to function as a city does in regard to the division of public and private space, variations in scale, texture, colour and material, and the complexity of massing and internal building typology.

The Dar il-Hanin Samaritan project in Santa Venera, Malta (1996), is a retirement home with its own chapel and facilities. In response to the practice of putting the elderly into sanitised and suburbanised settlements, the Dar il-Hanin Samaritan home uses a distinctively urban tectonic vocabulary, a series of structures set around a piazza, the twin foci of which are the chapel and the library/lounge. Elsewhere a complex composition of architectural elements creates a characteristically Mediterranean townscape of tightly knit units with simple, punched openings, together creating a series of confined spaces and screened interiors providing shelter from the harsh rays of the sun. The urban elements are in the process of being linked via a walkway to a garden of meditation, where a similarly urban approach leads to a garden of events, a scattering of pavilions and shading elements allowing the inhabitants to move from the confined to the open but keeping the two realms separate and thus avoiding the soul-destroying suburbanity that pervades most such institutions.

The University of Malta at Tal-Qroqq has been described as the last colonial building on the island. Designed in the early 1960s by the British firm Norman + Dawburn, it consisted of a number of rather unimaginative (although not bad for their period) masonry buildings clustered around a large, expressed auditorium building at the centre. The enormous expansion of the site, undertaken by Richard England in 1989, took nearly a decade to complete. It proved the ideal project for the architect to express his proclivity for treating buildings as minicities: it was in this scheme that he came as close to realising a new, virtually self-contained urban environment as is possible without embarking on the creation of a new city. The scheme is based around a series of terraced units, the spaces between which form an intricate network of ministreets. The larger units are punctuated by breaks and formal interventions which open up a hierarchy of vistas, glimpses (both of internal constructs and out to the natural topography of the site) and processional routes through the site in the vaguely picturesque tradition of Camillo Sitte. The site is modulated in three dimensions by steps, terraces, arcades, Zen-like rock gardens and formal, sculptural building elements. It is indeed the 'silence in between' which makes the site. The architectural expression of the built elements is simple: openings are merely punched through, inexpressive in the fashion of the Mediterranean vernacular, and the form of the blocks is unspectacular (occasionally evoking the repetitive grids and black openings of Aldo Rossi's eerie works), only catching the eye in rotated pavilions that break up the larger masses and in

Dar il-Hanin Samaritan, Santa Venera, Malta, 1996. *View of the courtyard and detached chapel screen*

brightly coloured cylindrical circulation elements. But in the arcades, gateways and passages there are echoes of Stirling, Botta and Rossi in the urban treatment of the linking spaces and the establishment of screens and colonnades which provide both the practical function of shade and the picturesque function of framing views and setting up formal geometries.

The Bab-al-Sheikh development in Baghdad dates from a much earlier phase in the architect's career (1982) and is on a huge scale. It was commissioned by Iraqi architect Rifat Chadirji (then consultant to the mayoralty of Baghdad), who also commissioned works by Ricardo Bofill, Arup Associates, Robert Venturi, Arthur Erickson and others as part of the same programme. One of the blocks was to be built around the existing Kheylani mosque, and the scheme was to provide exhibition and conference halls, restaurants and office space as well as housing. This building was positioned in a crescent plan embracing the domed mosque and creating a broad, curving promenade at the heart of the development. Shaded arcades were wrapped around the front of the mosque to shelter walkers from the harsh sun and to create a series of inviting public spaces. Work started on the development in 1984 but was soon abandoned.

A number of detailed designs for housing as part of the Bab-al-Sheikh development were also never realized. In its complex spatial treatment of the individual units, the adoption of local vernacular devices (screened bays, courtyards and set-backs to create terraces etc) and the recognition of the importance of the roofscape both as part of the broader urban picture and also as a traditional level of urban living (allowing activity and sleep under the stars and in the cool night air), England's scheme was conceived as a link between Arup Associates' contemporary modern typology and John Warren's rehabilitation of the old housing quarter. Much of the housing in the scheme was modelled on traditional domestic models. In this, much seems to have been learnt from the great master of Egyptian architecture, Hassan Fathy, and his follower Abdel El-Wakil who were prepared to acknowledge that international-style Modernism was rarely suited to the extremes of a desert climate and that all these traditional devices existed for good reason. The ridiculously wasteful, rootless and environmentally unjustifiable architecture of Abu Dabi, Jeddah or Las Vegas remains a testament to just how right Hassan Fathy and, in turn, Richard England were.

Fathy once said: 'A city is a civilised environment made up by man to represent the culture of a people as a group and to reveal its personality. It could be said that a city is cultural, social and economic form in space'.[4] This same description could be made of all of the above schemes and most of the others collected in this book. In the work of Richard England the city and the building are never quite separable but each is infused with the same humanity.

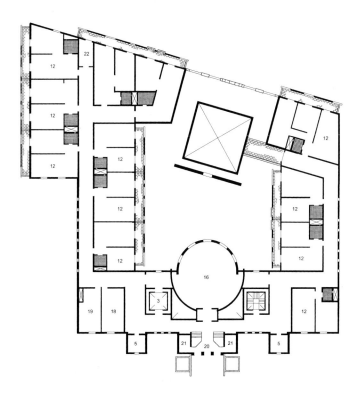

OPPOSITE TOP LEFT: Dar il-Hanin Samaritan, Santa Venera, *Threshold space at back of chapel*

OPPOSITE TOP RIGHT: Dar il-Hanin Samaritan, Santa Venera. *Doorway to the first floor terrace*

OPPOSITE BOTTOM LEFT: Dar il-Hanin Samaritan, Santa Venera. *View of the entrance to the chapel*

OPPOSITE BOTTOM RIGHT: Dar il-Hanin Samaritan, Santa Venera. *Internal courtyard with chapel screen-wall*

ABOVE TOP: Dar il-Hanin Samaritan, Santa Venera. *Ground floor plan: 3 Lift; 4 Staircase; 5 Toilets; 12 Units; 16 TV lounge; 17 Reception; 18 Administration; 19 Night nurse; 20 Entrance; 21 Telephone; 22 Store*

Notes

1. Lewis Mumford, *The City in History* (London: Secker &Warburg, 1961), p 576.
2. Edmund Bacon, *The Design of Cities* (London: T&H, 1974), p 19.
3. Peter Ackroyd, *London: A Biography* (Chatto & Windus, 2001)
4. Hassan Fathy, Paper, Al Azhar University, Cairo 1967.

Richard England

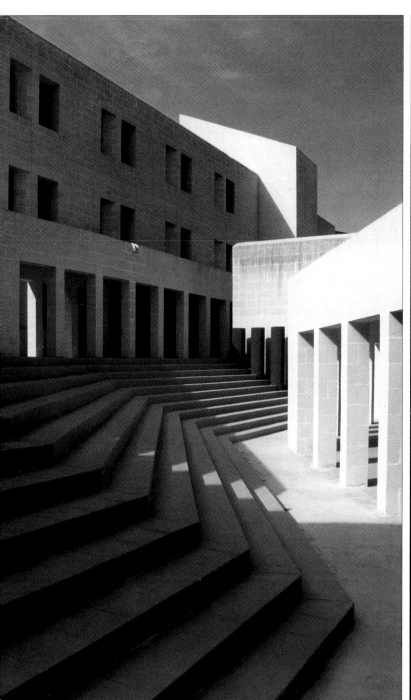

Opposite: University of Malta, Tal-Qroqq. *Detail of the main lecture hall*

Above left: University of Malta, Tal-Qroqq. *The Humanities block, the Silence in Between, Absence as a form of Presence*

Above right: University of Malta, Tal-Qroqq. *Architecture and Engineering Building*

Richard England

ABOVE: University of Malta, Tal-Qroqq. *The library sun screen*
OPPOSITE: University of Malta, Tal-Qroqq. *The library building*

Opposite: St James Cavalier Centre for Creativity, Valletta, 2000. *Atrium with bridge connecting to the lift tower*

Above: St James Cavalier Centre for Creativity, Valletta. *Concept sketch of the atrium*

Below: St James Cavalier Centre for Creativity, Valletta. *Section*

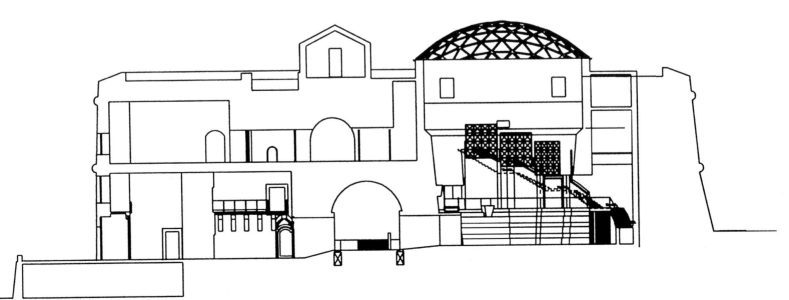

emphasising the equally important aspect to 'reach backward' in order to produce an architecture that, not only evolves *from*, but must also relate *to* 'the spirit of the place'.[7]

As well as these two defining buildings, England has been involved in designing major interventions that would dramatically alter the appearance, use and movement of people and traffic through Valletta. Among these are the designs for a new theatre on the site of the old opera house near the city gates. The original building was built by Edward Barry, architect of London's Covent Garden Opera House (and son of Charles Barry, architect of the Houses of Parliament), and it was a fine, if small, classical building, very much in the mid-nineteenth-century style but not in keeping with any of Valletta's highly developed traditions of architecture. Destroyed by bombing in the Second World War (in 1942), all that has remained since has been a part of the building's grand facade and podium, a doleful screen giving on to a car park. England's plans include the retention and restoration of the existing facade and the building of a dense, tightly packed building on the important site behind it. The plans also provide for a change of levels to arrive at Barry's original intentions for the facade proportions – the podium was a clumsy solution to a problem with the levels which occurred between the original design and the construction. The disposal of the podium would allow an easier flow between the street and the foyer, and England's intention is that the distinction between foyer and street should be broken down as far as possible, opening up the interior of the opera house through a transparent elevation.

As well as providing a substantial national theatre, the building would make sense of a currently unsatisfactory urban plan; filling in the unsightly gap would create an ordered and urbane environment in this pivotal public area. The theatre building itself is a monumental structure in the classical opera-house tradition. It would, in effect, have a number of main frontages including the one framed by the Barry facade, but also another defined by a massive stone elevation set within a larger glass framework. At points across the glazed curtain-walls England uses fragments of the language of the nineteenth-century opera house, or the Mediterranean palazzo, to pick out details, or important entrances or windows – an aedicule or a sliver of balcony may appear at any point on the elevations as a fleeting memory of what was on the site before – the final part of the plan to complete the rather unsatisfactory approach to this otherwise most coherent of European capitals.

At present the gateway to the city is defined by a bus station. Malta's ancient British buses may be one of its prime tourist attractions but the fumes they spew out and the chaos of trying to cross what is, in effect, a huge roundabout, by no means give the right impression of entry to this fastidiously planned city. In England's proposal the bus station is placed underground and manifested above ground in a glass structure that follows the shape of the original bastion. Its transparency would allow views to the original fortifications (or at least the foundations thereof) from the new piazza. By creating the ghost of the original, massive structures in glass, England plays on the change in meaning from an echo of a structure to defend in time of war to a structure intended to ensure public access and transparency in times of peace. These measures would also leave the entryway to the city clear of traffic and rationalise the bus routes which serve the city into a proper terminus.

The new piazza has been designed to incorporate the city gate and slender, elegant bridge designed for the site by Renzo Piano in the 1980s (and shamefully still unbuilt). The solidity of the elements used to create this new public space helps the landscape to blend into the bastions and fortifications. It also helps maintain the massive scale so that it still seems a slightly precarious journey to pass over the ditch from the echoes of the bastion through the break in the huge city walls over Piano's fragile bridge, which recalls the drawbridge that must have created the original link.

The huge wooden model of this proposed urban renewal makes clear exactly how far-reaching England's interventions into the fabric of historic Valletta have been and could yet be. By inserting the bank and the arts centre into two of the city's powerfully characteristic bastions he has revivified two formerly redundant structures, formerly redolent of war, siege and privation, and brought them into the public realm. The penetration and reinvigoration of these structures has opened up a whole new realm of the city, and opened the eyes of its citizens to the secret life and the ghosts of the past which remain in those massive fortifications. The creation of a new layer of history has profoundly enriched the city, and the links which would be made possible by the architect's urban proposals can only increase the clarity of both those interventions and the workings (in both a physical and metaphysical sense) of the city itself.

Notes
1. Joseph Paul Cassar (ed), (*St James Cavalier, Centre for Creativity*, Malta, 2000), p 13.
2. *Ibid*, p 18.
3. Jorge Luis Borges, RAI Italy, television interview, 1984.
4. Ben Okri, *Astonishing the Gods* (London: Phoenix, 1995), p 38.
5. Cassar (ed), *op cit* p 18.
6. Maurizio Vitta, *Richard England: The Spirit of Place* (Milan, L' Arca Edizioni, SPA, 1998), p 62.
7. *Ibid*.

OPPOSITE TOP LEFT: St James Cavalier Centre for Creativity, Valletta. *Theatre atrium with Victor Pasmore's 'Apollo 5' mural. Cast-iron columns are recycled from a 19th-century water cistern*

OPPOSITE TOP RIGHT: St James Cavalier Centre for Creativity, Valletta. *Layered 19th century stairs over 16th century gun ramp. New side-layer to carry service runs. Lighting structures are detached from original walls*

OPPOSITE BOTTOM: St James Cavalier Centre for Creativity, Valletta. *Intermediate floor layered over arches inserted in the original vaulted areas by the British in the 19th century*

Opposite: St James Cavalier Centre for Creativity, Valletta.
Staircase to theatre. Detail with layering of original cistern wall, marble and glass

Left: St James Cavalier Centre for Creativity, Valletta.
Music room: a metal structural system carries services and supports the acoustic panelling and ceiling structure

St James Cavalier Centre for Creativity, Valletta.
Cinema at first floor level

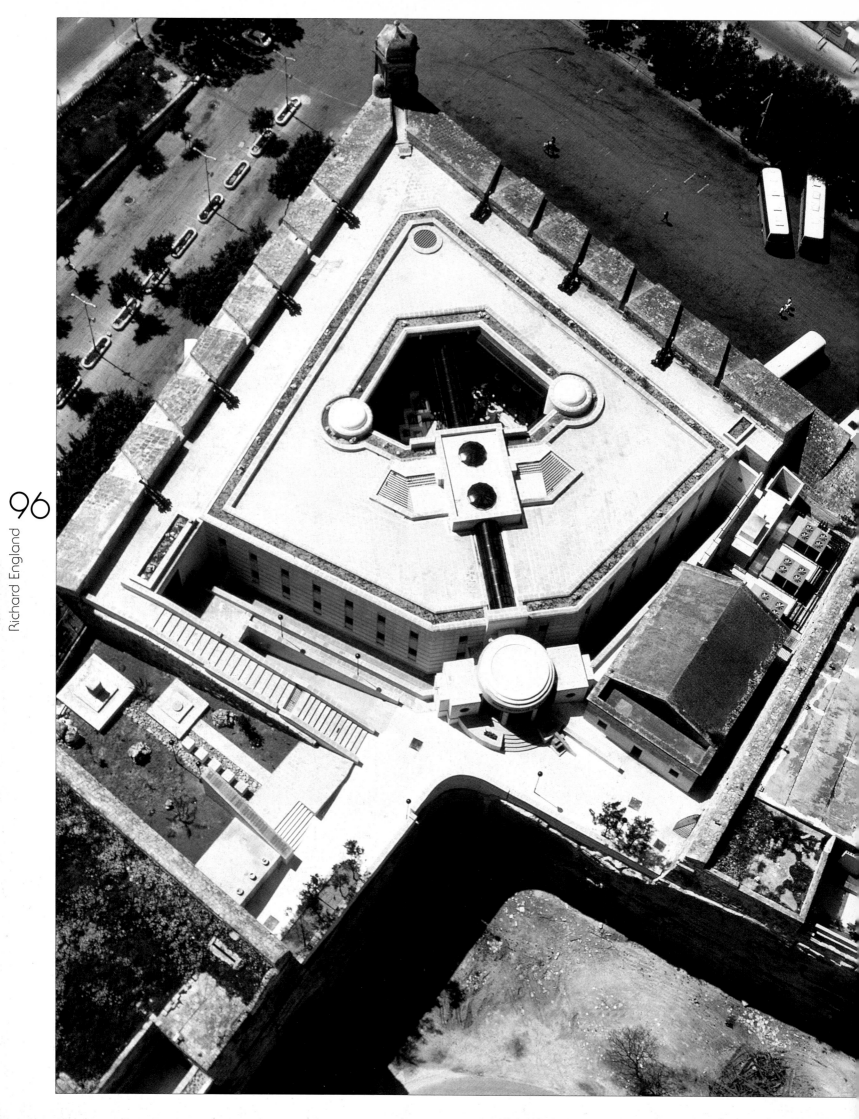

House for an Artist, Buenos Aires, Argentina, 1986

RIGHT, BELOW AND OPPOSITE: Church in Wroclaw, Poland, 1987